"The Marketing Secrets of a Multi-Millionaire Entrepreneur"

Jonathan Jay

*Practical Business Building Information
That You Can Use Today to
Accelerate Your Business Success*

D1136162

First published in Great Britain in 2008 by
SuccessTrack Business Training Ltd
202 Victory House
Somers Road North
Portsmouth
Hampshire
PO1 1PJ
Tel: 0845 029 7767
info@successtrackuk.com
www.successtrackuk.com

Edited by Marie-Louise Cook
Cover Design and typeset by ALS Designs, Portsmouth, Hampshire. Tel: 023 9283 1023

Printed and bound in Great Britain by
PPG Design & Print Ltd, Portsmouth, Hampshire. Tel: 023 9266 2232

British Library Cataloguing in Publication Data.
ISBN 978-0-9559701-0-8

CONTENTS

The most powerful copywriting formula ever created and how to use it NOW!

What turns readers into avid buyers?

The three deadly mistakes to avoid making in all your advertisements.

Why the length of your sales letter really does matter.

Your company's number one profit generator and how to make it work for you immediately.

How your database can save you a fortune in advertising.

Why knowing who isn't buying from you is crucial.

How to capture your best customer leads – easily.

Why you should go out of your way to encourage your customers to refer business.

Why waiting for word-of-mouth advertising kills business.

How to generate thousands more leads SUPERFAST!

How to use public relations to attract massive sales.

The most crucial fact to mention in any media interview.

The only website name you should ever use.

Why you don't need a Public Relations Agency to get great press coverage.

Why you should throw your press releases away.

The simplest way to raise your media profile.

How to become a published author without writing a single word!

*How a simple 'buy one-get one free' promotion could
make the biggest difference to your profit margin.
What you absolutely must have before you even think
of doing any promotion.
The promotion that always gets a huge response.
The secret ingredient every successful promotion contains.
What customers must get from you before they'll buy.
The one factor that virtually guarantees a response.*

*The no-cost way to attract thousands more customers.
How to massively accelerate your referral process.
The secret to unleashing an avalanche of referrals.
What to do when a customer compliments your product.
Why you only need six referrals to attract huge sales.
How to squeeze the most out of every referral you receive.*

*Why testimonials are the most powerful form of marketing.
How testimonials work – and why you must use them.
The very best time to ask for a testimonial.
Why sceptical customers write the best testimonials.
The key questions to ask to get a great testimonial.
How to add instant credibility to any testimonial.
How to use testimonials on your website to massively
increase sales.*

Chapter Nine   57
An Entrepreneur's Sales Secrets

Why you don't need a sales team.
The secret tool that is many, many thousands of times more effective than a sales team.
How to use a letter to motivate your potential customers to take action NOW!
How to guarantee only qualified prospects respond to your direct mail.
How to eliminate cold-calling forever!
How to provide personal contact to many people simultaneously.
How to get sales 24 hours a day, seven days a week without a sales team!

Chapter Ten   63
An Entrepreneur's Market Domination Secrets

Why size absolutely does not matter but why clarity is essential.
How to completely dominate your market - easily.
Why you must only focus on a portion of your market.
How to totally convince people they must have your products.
How to guarantee customers return again and again.
Why you should never sell the product – only its benefits.
How to position yourself as THE expert in your field and benefit!

PREFACE

When I started my business eight years ago, I had the princely sum of £145 to invest in it. At the time, I was getting daily phone calls from my bank… not because I was a valued client or they were interested in my welfare but simply because I owed them £50,000 and they wanted to know when I was going to repay it! My home was in danger of being repossessed and the telephone company was threatening to close my account and cut my telephone line. If I'd asked anyone "Is this a good time to start my own business?" they would have stated an emphatic "NO!!!"

"Forget it," they would have said. "Get yourself a proper job!"

They would have taken one look at my pretty dismal financial situation and made the prediction that the only result I could expect was failure. Fortunately, I didn't ask anyone. I used my £145 savings to set up a new industry in the UK. I started my company with a dream of changing people's lives and creating a profitable business. At the time, it was a completely new industry and over those eight years, it developed into something that is now taught in universities and top business schools. Last year, I was able to sell my company – the one set up with a meagre £145 – for millions of pounds. And I know that in the eight years I operated my business, I helped bring about enormous positive change in thousands and thousands of lives.

Along the way, I learnt the secrets of business success using a process known as 'trial and error'. I made some very costly mistakes. I advertised in expensive publications and didn't get a single response. I employed a huge sales team and watched as my profits were used to pay their wages. I invested in expensive office furniture and leased an overpriced office... I made many, many mistakes but I also learnt everything I needed to know about running a profitable business.

I used that knowledge to run marketing campaigns that drew in hundreds of thousands of pounds in just three days! I conducted a very successful public relations campaign (without spending a single penny!) and attracted thousands of new clients. I sold expensive study courses to many thousands of people - with the help of just one salesperson!

The secrets I learned weren't about the best ways to manage your bookkeeping or chase up invoices... they weren't about whether your computer system should run this or that system. In fact, you won't find anything about the mechanics of business administration in this book. No, what I am about to share with you are the crucial factors that determine whether your business will sink or swim. They are the factors that most businesspeople ignore because they are too scared to deal with them or worse, attempt but fail badly at... I'm talking about factors like sales, marketing, client attraction, client retention, lead generation, market domination, public relations, advertising... just the mention of these are enough to frighten most business owners but they are crucial to the success of any company. This book will provide you with the information you need to not only tackle all of these areas with true confidence but also absolute mastery.

It's only by mastering these areas that your business will truly prosper.

This book contains the basic principles, systems and strategies that will transform your business, your dream, your plan of a better life, into success. I have distilled what I learnt through expensive trial and error into something you can use immediately. It will save you years of costly mistakes... and save you from the risk of failure and the humiliation of having to give up your dream of running a successful business. It will accelerate your success... instead of something that could, should, maybe happen in years to come, you will be able to achieve a profitable business in a very short space of time. You will learn the secrets that only very, very successful entrepreneurs know and use. You don't need a degree from an expensive business school to understand them... they are straightforward, hugely practical and what's more... you can start using them immediately.

It's too easy to fall into the trap of believing that starting and running a successful business is an impossible dream. You deserve to fulfil your dream of living an independent life with a successful business. Follow the guidelines in this book and you will not only recession-proof your business and avoid the mistakes all too many business owners make but create a very, very profitable business... and enjoy yourself along the way!

Enjoy reading, but more importantly use these strategies in your business so that you can see the results for yourself.

I hope to meet you at a SuccessTrack event soon!

CHAPTER ONE
WHY SHOULD YOU LISTEN TO ME?

My name is Jonathan Jay and you may have seen me on the 'Midas Touch' panel at The Business Start Up Show, appear in their seminar theatre or even on the television advert for the show.

For the last eight years I have been introducing my business seminars by saying:

"The whole purpose of this seminar is to put more money into your bank account — guaranteed!"

Audiences often cheer when they hear that! Who doesn't want to have more money at the end of each month and year, more holidays and leisure time and a business that runs on autopilot?

You see, when I started in business I did it the hard way: I used **trial and error**, learnt from **my mistakes** and used **sheer persistence** to reach the breakthrough I was looking for. Then, with the benefit of hindsight, I realised that I had made life more difficult for myself than it had needed to be.

However, in eight years I went from being £50,000 in debt and having just £145 cash remaining in my embarrassingly small bank account to creating a coaching and training company from which I was able to draw an annual salary of a million pounds plus and sell for more millions last year.

I've shared my ideas on starting a business in my book ('Sack Your Boss!'), coached prospective business owners on TV's 'Now I'm The Boss' and spoken to thousands of business owners at The Business Start-Up Show. Now that I have sold my business I'm devoting my time to helping other business people achieve the success they are looking for.

My new business is called SuccessTrack and its sole purpose is to help <u>YOU</u> make more money, have more fun and free time and create a highly profitable business that can be sold – allowing you to do whatever you want for the rest of your life.

It all comes down to using the strategies, principles and systems that work (and which I'm about to share with you) to devise a business model that fulfils several criteria, so that your business is:

1. **Highly profitable**

2. **Sustainable**

3. **Constantly increasing in value and**

4. **A pleasure to own rather than a millstone around your neck!**

Follow the principles, strategies and systems in this book and your business will become:

Highly profitable

Your business will be highly profitable rather than just profitable. Too many business owners think that if you make a little bit of profit you can make it up in volume. However, that volume hardly ever comes, or it comes too late. You MUST aim to provide your product or service as profitably as possible.

Sustainable

Your business success will be sustainable, not a one-off, flash-in-the-pan experience. We all hear about business people who jump on the bandwagon and make money following the latest craze then disappear. You've probably seen shops that seem to spring up one day, last a couple of months, then close just as suddenly. That suits some people. I believe that it's far easier to create a business that is solid, resistant to market changes and creates profit month after month, year after year. That's what this book is about.

Constantly Increasing In Value

Your business will increase in value over time. It is will be an appreciating asset rather than one that stays static or worse, declines in value. Ultimately, you can take this appreciating asset and sell it, just like you might choose to sell your home.

Pleasurable

Your business will be a pleasure to run. Many business owners complain that the business runs them – rather than the other way round. I believe that it is completely possible to have a business that runs smoothly so that you can have a holiday without feeling guilty!

CHAPTER TWO
ADVERTISING SECRETS

As people become more immune to advertising, the importance of creating an advertisement that catches the attention of your target audience and encourages them to respond becomes vital. A bad advertisement vanishes into the background whereas a good one jumps out and grabs attention.

Entrepreneur's Advertising Secret #1
You don't need an advertising agency to create advertisements that sell.

Before creating your advertisement, clarify your objectives. Every advertisement should have an impact on sales from the day it is launched. Forget about the idea of using your advertisements to build awareness of your product or service. Brand building advertisements are an expensive luxury for small to medium-sized businesses. Your advertisements need to sell, sell, sell!

Entrepreneur's Advertising Secret #2
Keep all your advertising messages simple.

You need to clarify:

- What do you want to sell? Keep your offer simple: one product or one service. Offering too many products or services can confuse your audience.

- Who is your target audience? Where will you find them?

- How are you going to get the business? The use of special offers, promotions and incentives is becoming increasingly important. It gives people a reason to do business with you.

When you target your advertising, you know your audience and what they want to buy, and you know the words with which to connect to them, and which publications or media to use to reach them.

Entrepreneur's Advertising Secret #3
It's easiest to sell to the people who want what you have.

There are two categories of people:

1. People who are looking for what you offer and find you easily.

2. People who don't know what they want, don't know what you do and so need persuading and educating.

Make your life easier and focus your advertising on the first category of people – they are already converted and want the type of product or service that you offer and are ready to buy.

How Much Should You Spend?

How much money do you want to spend, what do you want to get for the expenditure and how are you going to measure the success of the advertising? Knowing what you want to achieve will determine the budget.

Entrepreneur's Advertising Secret #4
You are not selling a product or service but the solution to somebody's problem.

What Motivates People To Buy?

You need to do some market research. Find the people who will be buying what you have to offer. They will give you loads of free advice which can make your product or service better.

Understanding what people want and what motivates them to buy from you is absolutely essential. Most people don't understand what they are selling. They are selling solutions to people's problems.

You don't have to have the most sophisticated advertisements to have maximum impact. Simplicity and passion are more important than slick design.

Placing Your Advertisement

If you provide the filmwork for your advertisement rather than letting the publication design your advertisement, you have distinct advantages: you design the advertisement how you want it to look rather than how the publication wants it to look. Use a professional designer but make sure you tell them how you want the advertisement to look.

Design your advert with a heavy broken border rather than a straight line border. It will look like a coupon which will attract readers' attention.

Entrepreneur's Advertising Secret #5
Never accept the first quote. Nearly all prices are negotiable.

When you place your advertisement with a publication, ignore the price that appears on the website or on the 'rate card'. That is the sales department's Utopian ideal of how much they would like to achieve for the space available. As an entrepreneur, be prepared to haggle. Do not accept the first quote. Bargain and negotiate, especially as the closing date approaches! Begin by negotiating 50% of the rate card or even less.

The best position for your advertisement is always top right hand corner of a page and the worst is the bottom left hand corner. You'll probably need to ask for (or demand) the top right hand corner of the page.

How To Get People To Read Every Word Of Your Advertisement

Personalise your advertisement so that it talks directly to the right people (your target audience) in the right way. If you are advertising plumbing, for example, don't start with the name of your plumbing company. Begin with the solution to the problem that someone looking for a plumber would have.

You advertisement should encourage people to pick up the phone or place the order immediately. If your advert doesn't do that it hasn't worked. You must then decide whether to tweak it or advertise elsewhere.

Find out what works by asking the people who respond. Was it the 20% discount? Was it the headline? Was it the coupon? Use what they tell you to design your future advertisements.

Always test your advertisements this way. Ask the people who respond what enticed them to take action.

Entrepreneur's Advertising Secret #6
An insert is eight times more effective than a printed advert.

Inserts

An insert is a loose advertisement that is inserted between the pages of a publication rather than being printed on its pages. It captures the attention of readers and allows you flexibility in design and production. An insert can outlast the publication it appears in because people who are interested will hold onto it.

You can target only those readers who match your criteria. Don't worry about the large percentage of people who don't want or read the insert.

Inserts get a far better response rate than advertisements because magazines or newspapers limit the number of inserts that go into any one issue. (The weight of the inserts adds to the cost of the publication hence the limit on the number that are allowed in any one issue).

Entrepreneur's Advertising Secret #7
You need to give people a reason to respond to your advert.

Using Promotions In Advertisements

You need to give people a reason to respond NOW because once they turn the page, they will probably never return. You must seize the opportunity when you have it. It is essential to offer something that encourages people to pick up the phone or respond in some other way immediately.

To judge whether an advertisement has worked or not, it's essential to keep records. Keep track of the number of responses the advertisement creates and of course, the cost of the insert or advertisement. You need to know how long it takes people to respond, whether they respond best to newspaper, magazine or Internet advertisements and whether they prefer to place their orders online or pick up the telephone and call a number. You don't have to do this on an elaborate computer programme – if necessary, create your own record on paper.

Ask people where they saw your advertisement. Put in a code if you're running lots of different advertisements; it will make it easier to determine which advertisement people are responding to. From that, you'll be able to identify which advertisements work best and which ones you need to drop.

Conclusion

Advertising <u>does</u> work. You just have to advertise the right thing to the right people in the right way. Do that and you will have advertisements that help to really sell your product or service.

CHAPTER THREE

THE SECRET OF USING THE RIGHT WORDS

Copywriting is the art of writing words to create the outcome you desire (in the case of business owners, more sales). The words inspire potential customers (and existing customers) to take action – to pick up the telephone or to click the mouse button and order your product or service NOW. Copywriting is salesmanship in print.

> ## Entrepreneur's Copywriting Secret #1:
> *You are the best person to write about your product or service because you have the most passion, the most knowledge, and the most to win or lose.*

Writing advertising and sales copy is possible, no matter what your writing ability is. You don't have to be a writer to write good or even great copy. It doesn't matter if English wasn't your best subject at school. You are the best person to write about your product or service because as the business owner, you are the most passionate and knowledgeable about it. All you have to do is transfer that passion and information onto a page…

> ## Entrepreneur's Copywriting Secret #2
> *Customers only want to know what's in it for them.*

How To Write Great Advertising Copy
If you were sitting in front of me, what would you say about your product or service that would encourage me to buy it?

Would you wax lyrical or would you cut to the chase? Would you tell me about your company or would you tell me how your product or service would make my life easier and solve my problem? Hopefully, you'd focus on me – you'd know that I wouldn't care about how old your company was or how many staff you employed. All I'd want to know is how your product or service would solve my problem.

Get a tape or digital recorder then find someone to sit in front of you so that you can tell them what is so special about your product or service. (If you can't find anyone to do that, imagine I'm perched on a chair in front of you, about to race away. What can you say that will keep me in my chair?) Record your conversation. Once you've run out of things to say, take the recording and have it transcribed into a text document. That text document will contain the most persuasive advertising copy for your product or service ever. The next step is to take that rough copy and polish it so that it becomes a selling tool for you.

Now just edit it – take out the repetitions and the pauses and then you can use the copy on your website or in your brochure.

Entrepreneur's Copywriting Secret #3
People respond best to conversational writing styles.

Your copy needs to be conversational. The way to achieve that informality is to write as if you were speaking aloud. Too many businesses make the mistake of producing brochures or websites that contain very formal copy. People don't respond to it. They like the copy to be informal.

Entrepreneur's Copywriting Secret #4
AIDA is not only an opera but the most powerful copywriting formula ever created!

Your pages of copy might seem like a lot of random thoughts and ideas and there's a way of ordering it all that will transform it into a powerful sales tool using a formula called A.I.D.A. (Attention, Interest, Desire, Action). Your copy must begin with a statement that grabs your reader's attention. It must keep their interest so that they keep reading. It needs to arouse their desire for your product or service. And finally, it needs to contain a call to action.

The Most Powerful Copywriting Formula: AIDA

A: **Attention.** Get your customer's attention. How will your product or service solve your customer's problem?

I: **Interest.** Keep your customer's interest. Provide some more interesting information about how your product or service will solve their problem.

D: **Desire.** Arouse your customer's desire. Provide a powerful reason for buying your service or product.

A: **Action.** Tell your customer what action you want them to take. How do they order? Where do they order?

Entrepreneur's Copywriting Secret #5
Customers are not interested in your company, only in what your product or service will do for them.

How To Avoid Writing Bad Copy

The mistake many businesses make is writing about themselves. They focus on their company and the features of the product, how long they've been in business and how many awards they've won rather than what the product or service can do for the customer.

How To Write Amazing Copy

Go through your copy and check that it really does focus on your customer and their needs and wants. If you spot lots of references to 'we', 'us', 'our' or your company name, you need to rewrite it with your customer in mind.

> ### Entrepreneur's Copywriting Secret #6
> *Jargon, clichés, technical specs and humour will not clinch the sale. Simplicity will.*

Avoid using industry jargon. Leave out the clichés. Remove the technical specs. And forget about being funny: the majority of people probably won't get the humour. Keep the tone light and conversational.

> ### Entrepreneur's Copywriting Secret #7
> *No matter how long the copy is, it should always be interesting.*

How long should the copy be? Long copy is only effective if it's interesting. If your customer has no knowledge or experience of your product or service, your copy needs to inform, educate and persuade. The more complex the product or service, the more explanation it requires. However, the explanation needs to be interesting and understandable.

The danger with long copy is that it becomes long-winded. It becomes like the salesperson that doesn't shut up. The art of copywriting is knowing when to stop.

Conclusion

As a business owner, you are the best person to write about your company. You can do it! Keep your focus on your customer and how your product or service will solve their problems and your copy will become a very powerful sales tool that works 24 hours a day, seven days a week.

CHAPTER FOUR

LEAD GENERATION AND DATABASES

Why is it so important to have a database? Why collect customer and prospect information? The simple answer is if you have information on your customers you can look after them properly and you can return to them with new products and services.

Entrepreneur's Lead Generation & Database Secret #1

Your database is your most important asset and the key to your success.

The clever business owner knows the more information you have on people who are interested in your business – the more often you can return to them with additional offers. Just because someone doesn't buy today doesn't mean that your product isn't good, that your service isn't interesting or that they don't want it. It just means that they're not going to complete the transaction with you at this time.

Entrepreneur's Lead Generation & Database Secret #2

The more information you have about your customers, the more often you can contact them with additional offers.

Without a prospect database you have to continuously spend money to generate new leads. With a prospect database, you can return to old leads and enquiries and reactivate them.

Two of the biggest assets of any business are the customer database and the prospect database, the people who haven't yet purchased.

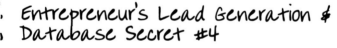

Entrepreneur's Lead Generation & Database Secret #3

A prospect database means you don't have to keep spending money to generate new leads.

Segmenting your database allows you to target the right message and the right offer to the right kind of people.

The more information you collect about the preferences of your prospects and customers – the more efficient and the more tailor-made you can make your offer.

Entrepreneur's Lead Generation & Database Secret #4

There are many ways to capture your customers' information.

You need multiple ways of getting people into your database. Direct Mail and the Internet are two obvious ones. Another is advertising in general magazines, newspapers or in the trade press.

You need to spend your advertising budget carefully and ensure you receive maximum returns for your expenditure. And you need to measure your investment regularly to determine how many leads become customers.

You need Direct Response Advertising – by which you can track the response. Your advertisement – whether it's press, radio, TV or outdoor - must encourage people to pick up the telephone and call your company or to visit your website. You need to stimulate the person who is reading, hearing or watching the advertisement to take action. You have to offer something which has sufficient value for that person to overcome inertia. Put a time limit on the offer (which might be a free CD; a free book; a free report; a free starter kit; free instructions; a free ticket; a free consultation; a free gift; or a free Mystery Gift).

In the trade press you can do inserts as well. An insert works eight times better than an advertisement because it's physical, it jumps or falls out, it's in the person's hands, and it's separate from the publication. The best combination is the advert in the publication plus the insert so you have a double-whammy. Give customers three response mechanisms: they phone, visit your website or fill in the card and freepost it to you. Free post - Comp-

Advertising in directories works very well too as does advertising in card decks (lots of inserts or postcards put together and mailed). Card decks are an excellent way of generating qualified leads.

Other ways of generating leads include going to events, running seminars and attending networking groups. In fact, anything you can do to get in front of customers will help generate leads. The more people you can get in front of through advertising, face-to-face contact or doing seminars, the better. You'll build your database and the database is the key to a successful business.

Entrepreneur's Lead Generation & Database Secret #5

A referred prospect is seven times more likely to buy.

Referrals don't cost anything and statistics show that a 'referred' prospect is seven times more likely to buy than a cold, unreferred prospect.

Entrepreneur's Lead Generation & Database Secret #6

Word-of-mouth advertising can be a slow way to generate sales.

The problem with word-of-mouth advertising is that it's dependent upon the amount that people talk. Your priority with your product, your service, and your business is to make it worthy of being talked about! You need to give everyone an irresistible reason to include your product, service or business in daily conversations.

Entrepreneur's Lead Generation & Database Secret #7

Joint ventures are an ideal way to generate new leads.

Joint Venturing can actually help the word-of-mouth referrals as well. When you look for a Joint Venture partner, look for a person who has the type of database that you want to tap into, and who has credibility, a great reputation and a willingness to participate.

Consider Joint Ventures with your competitors. People mistakenly assume that every other company in their industry is a direct competitor. But they're not. Why not get together with your competitors and share your unconverted leads?

On the Internet, two ways that you can leverage lead generation instantly are:

1. Joint Ventures and going to other people with similar websites.

2. Pay-per-Click – Having an advertisement that you pay for. On Google, you can get it up and running in 30 minutes – maybe even less sometimes – and you can be getting people clicking through to your website pretty much instantly.

You can go to Exhibitions and Trade Shows and generate leads. Someone else has done the hard work to get thousands of people interested in a certain industry or profession together and you have access to those thousands of prospects all for the price of renting a stand. To take advantage of the opportunity, you need to have something to give away to those prospects. You say, "Give me your details and I'll give you this." The giveaway must be irresistible. Then you have something more valuable than you could ever imagine: the details of several hundred people who are interested in your product or service.

Do the follow-up. Put their details on the database and categorise them. Focus on the people who do want what you have to offer.

What do you actually do with the data once you have it?

Get the information the person requested into their hands quickly. If you respond fast, people are impressed. Send something out in the post and then have Telesales follow-up. You get the edge on your competitors because they probably won't send it quickly and probably won't follow-up.

It's about building relationships with people who have asked to receive information from you. And then, it's about building that relationship over time.

Conclusion

Just because someone did not buy today does not mean they won't buy next year, the year after, or the year after that. You don't quite know when they're going to buy, but the database allows you to keep in touch – so that you have the opportunity to present your product, your service, over a period of time.

CHAPTER FIVE

PUBLIC RELATIONS

Public Relations (PR) means you and your business getting coverage (being written about in the media or being featured on the radio or TV). Why consider PR? It is a very effective way of attracting new customers and it reactivates old customers by rekindling their interest in your products or services. Does PR work? Absolutely.

Entrepreneur's Public Relations Secret #1

PR is an effective and inexpensive way to attract new customers and reignite the interest of existing customers.

Years ago, I used to advertise the courses run by my former company The Coaching Academy in the *Daily Mail* every Monday. It was a pretty small advertisement but was the most I could afford (about £400) and from that I would receive between 30 and 40 enquires every Monday or Tuesday. One week, a three page article about life coaching appeared and by a stroke of luck, my advertisement was placed at the end of the article. It looked as if my advertisement was linked to the article. That week, instead of getting between 30 or 40 enquiries, I had 700 so the effect of the advertisement was amplified enormously. By comparison, the person whom the story was about received no phone calls because there was no phone number at the end of the article. So if you are going to be interviewed or mentioned in an article make sure your company name and contact details appear in the article too.

Entrepreneur's Public Relations Secret #2

You must ensure every interview you do carries your contact details.

There is nothing worse than doing a great interview and then receiving no phone calls, no sales or orders. Normally, a journalist won't allow you to include your telephone number at the end of the article so what can you do? Make sure you state your company name as a web domain name. For example, if I was being interviewed and wanted to promote my company, I would say, 'I'm Jonathan Jay and I'm from **successtrackuk.com**' It would mean my website address would appear in the article so even if the journalist or publication refused to publish my contact details at the end of the article, they would have to mention my company name (which is my website address) in the article.

Entrepreneur's Public Relations Secret #3

Make it easy for people to find you on the Internet – create a website using your name.

Another way people find you is to enter your name into an Internet Search Engine. The only guaranteed way of ensuring that someone finds you on the Internet is to run some advertising with a Search Engine like Google. Ensure your name is also a domain name. For example, Jonathan Jay becomes **www.jonathanjay.com** so that if anyone enters 'Jonathan Jay' the Search Engine locates the website which has the greatest relevance to that enquiry.

People respond more to something that a publication has written about you than something you have written yourself. It's generally accepted that you've written the advertisement and the publication has written the editorial. The hybrid of this is called 'the advertorial' which looks like something factual the publication has written but is in fact something you have written or paid to have written. It's so deceptive and works so well that publications often put at the top of the advertorial 'Advertising Feature' so that readers understand they are reading a form of advertising editorial.

Entrepreneur's Public Relations Secret #4
You do not need to use a PR agency to attract great publicity.

How To Get Good PR

There are two routes to getting good PR: DIY or employing a PR agency to do it for you. My experience of paying someone to do my PR has not been a good one. I have wasted an absolute fortune with PR companies that promised so much and never delivered. So my advice is: don't pay for PR because you can do it yourself and no-one else will have such a vested interest in promoting your company as you do.

How? It's easy. Pick up the telephone and talk to the media. If you feel uncomfortable doing it, ask someone else – a close relative or friend who has good communication skills. Make sure you sit there as it happens. Talk to your local media representatives: local newspapers, magazines, and radio and television stations.

Entrepreneur's Public Relations Secret #5
Forget about press releases – good journalists won't use them.

Why You Don't Need Press Releases

Books about PR will urge you to send press releases but I believe this is wrong. Good journalists ignore press releases. They will pay attention to a list of bullet points that you have mailed, faxed or emailed in and which cover the salient points of your story. You need to find a journalist who can see the story within those bullet points. If you can't sum up your story in those six or seven bullet points, no-one else will understand it. The story won't happen.

One of the easiest ways to get your story picked up by the media is to link it to something that's already in the press. Another simple way to get media coverage is to be controversial (just make sure your controversial story is a positive one!)

The most obvious story is that you are starting a business. What if your business is similar to existing businesses? Focus on what sets your company apart from the others.

Right now, there is a lot of admiration for entrepreneurs. Think of the popularity of the TV programme, **'Dragon's Den'**. You can tell the media that you were inspired to start your own business after watching **'Dragon's Den'**. That's a story.

Paul Hartunian's story ('The Man Who Sold The Brooklyn Bridge') illustrates that if you are willing to put in the hard work and keep your eyes open for opportunities, they will appear in front of you. You need to find the angle that makes your story different.

Entrepreneur's Public Relations Secret #6

Write a book or report – it's the easiest way to raise your profile.

How To Raise Your Profile: Write A Book

One of the easiest ways to get a media profile is to be published. Self-publishing is as valid as being published by a mainstream publisher. How do you write a book if you are not a natural writer? Write down lots of questions that people have asked about your business in the past. For example, 'How do you get started in this business?' 'What tips do you have?' 'How do I choose the best product/service?' 'How much should I expect to pay?' 'How do I choose the right person to do the job?'

Have the questions in front of you and record your answers into a tape or digital recorder. Have the recording transcribed into a text document (using a secretarial bureau). Once you have the text document, make any corrections that are necessary. If you'd prefer to have someone else do the writing and editing for you, visit **www.elance.com** and find an editor. Have the document typeset (again, you can find someone to do this at **www.elance.com** or in your local area). Then find the designer to create your book cover.

Entrepreneur's Public Relations Secret #7
You don't need amazing writing skills to write a book or report – you can pay other people to create it for you.

You don't need any publishing expertise to create your book, booklet or report. All you need to do is to transfer the knowledge you have to a tape or digital recording format. Once you've done that, the rest is easy.

You'll find doors open and opportunities abound once you are a published author. It happened to me and it can happen to you too.

Conclusion

Don't believe the hype: public relations does not have to be tricky or expensive. You can do your own public relations – you don't need to employ the services of a PR agency. You don't need to be a great writer to attract the attention of the media – you just need to have a good story (or a new angle on an existing story)!

CHAPTER SIX

PROMOTIONS THAT BRING YOU MORE SALES

Promotions stimulate activity. They give people an incentive to try your services or products and they set your company's products or services apart from the competition. Your promotion should be so exciting, worthwhile and enticing that potential customers feel compelled to take immediate action.

Entrepreneur's Promotions Secret #1
Promotions stimulate sales activity.

Why have promotions?

It might be a time of year when traditionally your sales dip. Maybe you have an over-supply of stock. Perhaps you want to counteract someone else's promotion. Or the competition is hotting up so much that you need your products or services to stand out. You might want to acquire new leads and customers.

Many business owners consider promotions to be gimmicky or risky and believe they are only appropriate for supermarkets. Those business owners are missing a massive opportunity for business growth. Remember, airlines do promotions. No-one says British Airways is 'tacky' because it does a 'two for one' promotion. Harrods, the department store, does promotions and Harrods is certainly not tacky.

> ## Entrepreneur's Promotions Secret #2
> *To make a promotion financially viable, you must have additional products to up-sell.*

What you must consider before a promotional giveaway

Giving a product or service away – free of charge – is a very fast way of generating business but if you don't have any other products or services to sell to those customers, you've just generated costs for your company that you might never recover. You must have a back-end product to sell to those 'free sample' customers to recover the huge cost of providing those enticements in the first place.

Having the infrastructure to support the promotion is vital. It has to stack up financially and it has to be logistically manageable. That doesn't mean you have to suddenly employ 20 extra staff in your office: you can manage a large-scale promotion even if you're a one-person business.

It takes courage to do a promotional campaign and you will need to calculate your risk. You will have to ask, "If we do this – is anyone going to pay us? If they do pay us – are we going to have enough money to keep going?"

> ## Entrepreneur's Promotions Secret #3
> *The most popular and therefore successful promotions are the 'buy one, get one free' variety.*

Types of promotions

Price promotions are the most obvious type of campaigns and three of the most popular are:

'Two for One'

You get two of whatever it is for the price of one – so you get two car washes for the price of one, for example.

'Buy one, get one free'

Buy one product and receive the other product free of charge.

'Half Price'

If you buy a product, you only have to pay half the normal price.

Out of the three, the most successful is the 'Buy one, get one free' – and that proves that people don't necessarily buy on price. They would rather have something of additional value than something half price.

With a 'buy one, get one free' promotion, you're not cutting the price; you're actually giving something additional away. Price cutting maybe the first promotion you consider but be careful because it can devalue your customers' perception of your product or service.

Other Promotions To Consider

You could do promotions where you leave the price as it is but change the method by which people pay. For example, if you have always demanded payment up-front, offer a staggered payment plan. If you have only ever accepted cheques, accept credit cards as well. You can time delineate that and say, "For the next two weeks, any new customer can spread the payments over the next six months - interest free."

'Try before you buy' is a great way of allowing people to sample what you do. It's very reassuring. Allow people to experience it and then say, "If you like what you experience, you pay. If you don't like what you experience, then you don't pay." It's as simple as that.

Entrepreneur's Promotions Secret #4

For a successful promotion you need an irresistible offer.

Competitions and surveys are very effective promotional techniques too. Combining and packaging things together make a great promotion. It's about building value. This is the key to a successful promotion – creating an irresistible offer. This is the goal – creating something that someone would have to be stupid to walk away from.

You can partner with other companies so you run promotions for each other. You can combine the joint venture with a promotion – and that's very, very powerful too.

Entrepreneur's Promotions Secret #5

When done well, the 'refer a friend' promotion boosts your customer base enormously and enhances the company's profile.

The refer-a-friend type of promotion is often considered boring but if it is done properly, it can really boost the growth of your customer base.

When you promote something as 'new', 'first time in the UK' or that has 'never been seen before', you create an element of excitement, buzz and mystery which is very important. It also stimulates word-of-mouth advertising, which brings enquiries into your database.

All of these things are intrinsically linked. If you can do all of these things and get them working together – you don't have to have a particularly clever plan to get them working together, just do them and watch them all start to integrate – then you will find that your business will grow and grow and grow. It will happen so much quicker than if you simply took a passive approach to your business.

Entrepreneur's Promotions Secret #6
Provide a reason for doing the promotion to build customer trust.

Why You Need To Explain To Your Customers

You must provide your customers with an explanation about why you are doing the promotion.

Giving a reason 'why' helps customers to see that the company can slash prices and still operate. You have to say: "The reason why we can drop the price here is because…" It doesn't have to be a complicated reason. It can be: "It's my birthday and I thought I'd send an extremely special, fun, birthday offer."

It builds that trusting relationship within your loyal customer group because they feel included. They know why you're doing the promotion.

Entrepreneur's Promotions Secret #7
A time limit creates a sense of urgency and virtually guarantees a response.

The Key To A Successful Promotion

You must add a time limit to your promotional offer if you want it to really succeed. Tell people what they need to do and how little time they have left to do it.

Conclusion

Creating a powerful, compelling and absolutely irresistible promotion is the key to differentiating yourself in a market – however crowded it may be – and if you can do that, then you have something unique… your business success is completely assured.

CHAPTER SEVEN

REFERRALS

How To Get New Customers At Little Or No Cost

A referral is someone else doing your sales and marketing for you at no cost and because they want to. Their experience of your product or service was so positive they want to share it with other people.

What are the drawbacks? If you rely on word-of-mouth referrals, your business will only grow at the speed at which other people talk. If your business offers products or services that people don't necessarily talk about (or want to talk about) like counselling, then word-of-mouth will be a slow method of growth for you. If your customers don't regard your products or services to be very exciting or interesting then word-of-mouth referrals may be slow.

Entrepreneur's Referrals Secret #1
Speed up the referral process by asking for them.

If your product or service lets someone down, then they will talk about it in a negative way.

Before you ask for referrals ensure that the product or service you offer is regarded in a positive way by your existing customers. It should delight rather than merely please.

To speed up the process, ask your customers for referrals. Have your customers out there telling everyone they know about your product or service. The only way they will do that is if you encourage them. The encouragement can be as simple as a request that they refer a friend.

Tell people what you would like them to do. Referrals are cost-effective and they do work. It is seven times easier to sell to a referral than to a brand new customer because the person who did the referral has already convinced the friend that doing business with you makes sense. They have been pre-sold.

Entrepreneur's Referrals Secret #2
Generate tons of referrals by doing something extraordinary.

How To Get Lots Of Referrals
The easiest way is to do something that is so extraordinary people can't help talking about it. Think of something you can do that makes it intrinsically conversation-worthy.

Give people a reason to talk about your business, product or service. It has to be a reason that isn't completely self-serving to you. People won't mind helping you to build your business if they have had a good experience but they're not going to go out of their way to do it. Why should they?

Entrepreneur's Referrals Secret #3
How you ask for referrals makes all the difference.

The Art of Getting Referrals
The art of getting lots of referrals lies in the way you ask for them. If you say, "Do you know anyone else who might enjoy my product/service?" people will say they'll have a

think and let you know. The chances are they will forget the question once they've left your premises. So be specific and be direct. Ask, "Who do you think will benefit from my product/service?" When they tell you, ask them specifically where you can find those people (their company, industry, or within the organisations, clubs, groups or networks they belong to).

Entrepreneur's Referrals Secret #4

When a customer compliments your products, ask if you can quote them. Write it down, read it back to them. Use it.

Another way of getting referrals is to build a bank of testimonials. A testimonial is a third party endorsement. It's somebody else saying you are good rather than you saying you are good. Capturing testimonials is quite an art form. People are busy so you need to make it easy for them. You need to prompt your customers. When they tell you what a great service/product you have and what a great impact it has had on their lives ask them if you can quote them on your website/brochure etc. Jot down what they've said. Read it back to them. Ask if you can use their name and title and their industry. Tell them you'll send them a copy of the brochure or a link to your website so they can see how it appears.

Entrepreneur's Referrals Secret #5

Detailed testimonials about different aspects of your products and services work best.

You don't need to have hundreds of testimonials – six is enough so long as each one says something positive about a different aspect of your product or service. One might be about your customer service, another about the quality of the product or service, another about the speed of delivery and after-care service you provide, and another about the efficiency of processing the orders. Those testimonials become an army of unpaid salespeople working for you 24 hours a day, seven days a week.

Entrepreneur's Referrals Secret #6
Keep updating your testimonials. Collect new ones regularly.

It's important to refresh and update your testimonials often.

Strategic Testimonials
Offer testimonials to other businesses. For example, offer to write a testimonial for a company that you have dealt with and been happy with. Suggest you include your photograph, title and company name and a link to your web address with your testimonial and that it be placed on the other company's website homepage. It means every person who visits that website sees your face, company name and reads your positive comments. Every company that uses your testimonial is effectively promoting you and your product or service.

Get testimonials every day. Don't just ask for referrals once every quarter. Make it part of your everyday routine. If you encourage your customers and clients to do referrals, the people they send are already in the mindset of referring. They will refer other people.

Entrepreneur's Referrals Secret #7
Make the most of your customer feedback – use it on your brochures, website, in CD format and on telephone recordings.

How To Maximise Your Referrals

It's very simple to set up a recording device in your office. When customers say something positive about your product or service, ask them to repeat it into the microphone. Explain you're putting together a short compilation CD of people saying how your company has helped them. Alternatively you could hold a 'Customer Appreciation Day' and invite all your customers to come to your office... offer free refreshments and thank them for their loyalty and business. Have someone there with a microphone to record their positive comments. Send all the recordings to an audio editor (you can find them on the Internet). You will then have a CD of people saying nice things about your product, service and company. You can send that CD to your potential customers (people who have enquired but not yet purchased).

You can set up an 0800 phone number that plays that CD... put the phone number on your website, in your brochure or on your business card and says "Dial this number free of charge and listen to what our customers say about us". Your customers will once again be your (unpaid) salespeople. They will be referring your product or service to people they don't even know.

CHAPTER EIGHT

TESTIMONIALS

One of the most powerful things you can do when you are marketing your business product or service is to show that it does what it's meant to do. If it's a product – does it work? If it's a service – does it provide what people want?

Entrepreneur's Testimonials Secret #1

Testimonials prove to potential customers that your product or service has value.

The easiest way to do that is to have testimonials from people who have bought your product or used your service. Testimonials provide the social proof that other people have bought your product or service, taken the risk, tried it out and found it to be of great value.

Most people don't use testimonials effectively and don't see the impact they can have. They don't even see the necessity of collecting testimonials from clients. But if you get the right testimonials from the right people, it builds respect, prestige and your professionalism. It elevates you in the eyes of the person reading the testimonial. They say, "Well, if this person says she's good – she must be good!"

Entrepreneur's Testimonials Secret #2

Testimonials build confidence and enhance respect for your company.

Now, if the person whose opinion counts says, "Don't like it", say: "I am going to impress you so much. I'm going to go away to remodel and recreate my product. I'm going to improve it and I'm going to come back to you in four weeks time and ask for your opinion again." In four weeks time, you return and they say, "You know something? That is absolutely amazing" and that endorsement will probably end up stronger that it would have been originally.

Entrepreneur's Testimonials Secret #3

Ask for the testimonial immediately after the customer expresses a positive response.

When do you approach somebody for a testimonial? The best time to ask for it is when that person has just experienced your product or service and is feeling good about it. If they say immediately after using your product or service, "This is the best thing I have ever bought!" you should say, "That is such a compliment – could I put that on my website?"

You must get that testimonial immediately (before their euphoria disappears) – ideally in writing then use it on your website, your business card, your brochure and at the end of your emails.

Writing testimonials can be quite difficult for people so you have to help them. You go to your computer and you write: "Hi, You said to me that our product 'is the best you have EVER had'. Is it okay if I quote you saying this on my website? Just whip me back an email if it's a 'Yes'."

They reply and say: "Yeah, go ahead!"

Fantastic – there's your testimonial. You've actually done the hard work for them.

The key is to get testimonials about different aspects of your service or product. Think of it as a CAT scan – providing clarity from every single angle and providing absolute transparency so there is zero doubt in the prospect's mind that buying your product or trying your service will be the best decision they ever made.

Entrepreneur's Testimonials Secret #4

One of the most powerful testimonials is the one in which the customer admits they were hesitant or sceptical but is now converted.

What makes a good testimonial? It doesn't have to be entirely positive. A good testimonial can actually begin in a negative vein (and obviously finish in a positive one) because it shows a change in attitude and highlights the sort of thoughts and doubts that other prospects might have.

Don't use testimonials that just say "Fantastic!" etc. They don't really have any weight. Similarly, don't just feature someone's initials at the end of the testimonial. You need to build up the layers of detail and you need the person's full name, their title, their location (for example, London, UK) and their job title with a description of their job function (for example, CEO or IT Manager).

Entrepreneur's Testimonials Secret #5

Ask for your customer's full name, job title and industry.

When people see that they say, "Hey, I'm an IT Manager. That person's an IT Manager – they loved it. So will I." So, you're building rapport through the printed word. You also need their Industry and Profession, for example, IT Manager in the frozen food industry. It could be translated into the kind of consumer market. It might say, "Jenny, Mum of two – I loved this product, my kids loved it."

Then you add a date. If your testimonials are more than a year old, you get new testimonials. You should collect testimonials and rotate them all the time.

Entrepreneur's Testimonials Secret #6
A photograph of your customer adds further credibility to the testimonial.

You should also add a photograph of the person giving the testimonial. It's all about building credibility and making it believable so the social proof just gets stronger. It helps to build rapport because it shows that you understand people like them, and people like them are already buying from you.

If you have hundreds of testimonials collected on your database and you know the professions of those people, you categorise them. On your website, have a drop-down menu that says, "Find your occupation here" and let's say a teacher is looking, he or she clicks on the 'Teacher' section of the menu and there are your teacher testimonials. You are connecting your testimonials with a person, rather than leaving it to chance.

You can also use video and audio testimonials on your website or you can put them all onto a CD and send it with your initial information pack and say, "Don't take our word for it, listen to what our customers have to say."

Entrepreneur's Testimonials Secret #7
Use audio and visual testimonials on your website.

The people who listen to it are the people who need and want the additional proof. It's worth it for the very small amount that it costs to produce a CD. You could put those on your website too – "Click here to play" and there they are. You can do exactly the same with video – you can put it onto a DVD or onto your website, so people can see video testimonials on your web site. People like to see things, or hear things or be able to read things to get a sense of what a product or service is like. If you can put video and audio on your website – you're appealing to all of those senses.

The case study is typically longer than a testimonial and it takes a particular set of circumstances and shows a journey where the use of the product or service is transformational in some way.

The essential elements of both case studies and testimonials are: credibility, believability, variety and an endorsement of your product or service. If you have good testimonials and good case studies, you make it so much easier for potential customers. You lower the barrier.

Conclusion
If you add in the right testimonials and the right case studies to support what you provide in your business – will it make a difference? Absolutely it will make a difference. In fact, you'll wish you'd done it years ago!

CHAPTER NINE

SELLING WITHOUT HAVING A SALES TEAM

If you want to increase the sales of your product and service you don't have to employ a sales team do it. There are other ways of doing it which produce the same (or even better) results with less effort, less money, and less stress.

Entrepreneur's Sales Secret #1
You don't need a sales team, just effective marketing.

How? It's easy. You let your marketing do all the work. Think of it this way: salespeople can only talk to a certain number of people a day. They have off-days and they have on-days. There are many reasons why salespeople have suppressed sales. However, your marketing can be multiplied and replicated thousands of times without having to hire thousands of people.

Let me give you an example: If you want to sell your product or service to a potential customer, you (or your salesperson) have a conversation that lasts at least 10 minutes either over the telephone or in person. Your potential customer might be interested and might buy it. They might not but you (or your salesperson) will still spend 10 minutes in conversation, regardless of the outcome. In a day, there are only so many 10-minute conversations you (or your salesperson) can have.

What if you wrote a letter to that potential customer instead? How about if your letter was sent not just to one potential customer but 1,000 or 10,000 or even 100,000 of them? In fact, what about if your letter was sent to as many people as you can find who might be interested in your product or service?

Entrepreneur's Sales Secret #2

A direct mail letter will deliver the same message to thousands of targeted customers at the same time.

By using direct mail, you can contact many people with the same sales message. Your potential customers all read it within the same 24-hour period and react. They say, "Okay, do I want it? Or don't I want it?" In fact, up to that point, it's the same as if you were right in front of each of those people! If they are interrupted, they can return to your letter later on. They can pass your letter onto other people – which they can't do with a telephone call.

Entrepreneur's Sales Secret #3

A successful direct mail letter encourages potential customers to take action immediately through the use of incentives.

You offer them a huge incentive to take action, to make the purchase or the booking. What are the kinds of offers and promotions that would stimulate a list of prospects to get in touch with you?

- Time limited – phone today

- Claim something free

- Add in a bonus gift

- A special offer

- A 'buy one - get one free' promotion

- Something that's running out.

What you're looking for is a promotion that creates action NOW – rather than later.

In your letter, you've explained what they need to do. "If you want this, this is what you do; pick up the phone and call this number, and speak to one of our team." One number, one person.

You've told them what sort of person makes an ideal customer. "You are perfect for this product if you fulfill these criteria. But if this is you… this, this, this – no way, it's not for you."

Entrepreneur's Sales Secret #4
You can use a direct mail letter to ensure only qualified prospects call you.

It means you'll only be speaking to qualified prospects – people who've read what you do, know how much it costs, and who fulfil the criteria. They phone you and say, "I'm interested!"

"Fantastic! Well, what else would you like to know?" You've already answered all of the questions they may have about the content of the letter – because you also put in a Frequently Asked Questions (FAQs) sheet. Usually, all people want is to hear a nice voice on the end of the phone that says, "How can I help you?"

Once you have that personal relationship – they either buy, or they don't buy. If they don't buy, something's gone tragically wrong since the phone was answered.

Entrepreneur's Sales Secret #5
A direct response letter means you only need someone to answer the telephone to take orders.

All you need is someone responding to the phone calls at your end. If you don't have anyone, if you're a one-person business – either it's you doing it or a call centre and they take all the calls, take the messages and email them to you, and then you can respond to them one after the other.

Compare that to your army of telesales people phoning out and speaking to possibly two people that qualify in a day. I'm sure you'd rather have one person accepting incoming calls from qualified prospects than an army of salespeople making phone calls to unqualified prospects.

And as a business owner, you'll agree that managing one person who takes incoming phone calls is far less stressful than managing a team of people!

Now, many businesses choose to have a sales force because they feel the need for personal contact and to build a relationship. If you're adamant that your product or service can only be sold voice-to-voice then use this technique: use the direct sales letter to drive people to a teleconference in which someone highly qualified (you, your best salesperson, one of your presenters, trainers or your Managing Director) talks about the product for 40 minutes in a sufficiently interesting way and then answers questions.

Entrepreneur's Sales Secret #6

Offer clients who want personal contact access to a teleconference led by one of your company representatives.

The questions will be from people who have been interested enough to pick up the phone and listen for 40 minutes – so they won't be tricky questions! Your spokesperson answers the questions and then offers callers a very strong incentive to take immediate action. "Phone in the next hour to buy and you'll receive..." Which means every time that phone rings it's a sale!

Entrepreneur's Sales Secret #7

It's all about removing the necessity for employing huge numbers of people and making a process that you can do at any time on any day of the week. The alternative is to have a big sales floor with dozens of people making outgoing phone-calls, massive phone bills, huge wages and very high stress levels.

Once you have that system there, you only have to tweak it occasionally if circumstances change. Keeping an eye on the system is easy compared with keeping an eye on a team of human beings.

So you:

1. Send someone a letter

2. Drive them to a teleclass

3. Send them an email

4. Do a voice broadcast.

Combine those four things and you have an automatic Business Creation machine.

Conclusion

It is possible to sell more of your product or service using an automated system that works 365 days of the year. It's easy and it works!

CHAPTER TEN

DOMINATING YOUR MARKET

Dominating your market doesn't mean you have to be the biggest in a particular industry, profession, or marketplace. Being smaller sometimes allows you to be more agile than larger companies. If you're going to play to win however you want to be the most successful business in your marketplace and there are certain things that you can do to position yourself in that way.

Entrepreneur's Market Domination Secret #1

Size is not important. Clarity is essential.

It's a lot easier to dominate your market if you're very clear about what your market is. Who are your customers? People who believe everyone's a customer have a hard battle on their hands. To have a generic product which suits everyone is difficult because:

• You have such a large marketplace you don't know where to start.

• You can never specialise.

• You can never become expert in a certain field.

Entrepreneur's Market Domination Secret #2

Niche your product or service and market domination becomes very easy.

If you have a specific niche market for your field, your product or service, it becomes extremely easy to become the leader in that marketplace.

When you niche your product or service several things happen: you know where to focus your marketing and where to find your customers. When you do that, you become expert in that marketplace because:

- You have the same type of customers

- You're providing the same service or product

- You become better and better at what you do.

You increase the referrals you receive because when you are an expert people will refer you to others. When you are an expert in your niche your charges increase because people are willing to pay more for an expert than a generalist.

Entrepreneur's Market Domination Secret #3

Focus solely on the customers that bring in most of your income.

It can be more profitable for a business to cut out some of what they do and focus on one particular area. Typically, 20% of your income is provided by 80% of your customers, and 80% of your income comes from 20% of your customers. It means most of your business income derives from 20% of your customers so focus solely on them. When you focus on those people – you will attract other people like them because those 20% say, "This business only specialises in people like us."

Creating a segment of the market gives you the power to dominate that market. People pay money and go straight to that one place because it provides the product or service they want. You need to position your company as the only place to go.

> ## Entrepreneur's Market Domination Secret #4
> *Educate your customers about why they should buy your product or service.*

Part of this involves education: if people don't know about your company and its specialist products or services, they're not going to buy from you. You need to educate your customers as to why you are the expert. You do that by determining what makes you an expert. Is it because:

- you have more experience?

- you have staff that have more experience?

- you have been in the business longest?

- you have the biggest range?

- you have exclusive supplies?

- you can do special orders?

- you provide an unsurpassed service?

You're not just taking money from your customers in return for a product or service – you're also providing backup and a support mechanism that they won't find elsewhere. You're offering all of those things. By doing this you attract a clientele to your business that wants the best. And you know something? They're the best customers because they appreciate you more.

Entrepreneur's Market Domination Secret #5

Determine what your customers want from you and surpass their expectations.

Being specific about who your customers are is the first step. One way to find out is to survey your customers. Ask them:

1. What should we start doing?

2. What should we stop doing?

3. What's just right?

4. What should we do more of?

5. What should we do less of?

Offer people an incentive to complete and return the survey.

Entrepreneur's Market Domination Secret #6

Sell the benefits of your product or service.

Focusing on the benefits rather than the features does help people to understand why they should pay that little bit extra for your product and service. It's positioning you away from simply offering a commodity that everybody's offering to offering something special. It says you really understand your customers and what they actually want. It's no longer about a commodity: it's a service and a product combined.

Ideally, you want to move away from a transactional relationship – the sort you have with your supermarket: you give them money and take your groceries.

Part of the key to that is actually:

- Capturing the details of the people who are visiting your website

- Understanding what they're buying, and

- Being able to predict their buying habits.

Entrepreneur's Market Domination Secret #7

Let your customers know that you are an expert in this field.

There are other ways of positioning yourself in the marketplace. One of the fastest ways to position yourself at the top of your marketplace is to be an author. If you have written a book then people automatically perceive you as an expert. You become a trusted advisor.

When you position yourself in your niche, you become far more focused in your marketing than you could ever do if you were just being a generalist. It opens up so many opportunities.

Once you've dominated one niche – you can develop a second niche. But again, select a niche rather than trying to be all things to all people.

Conclusion

- Decide who your customers are or who you want them to be and focus on dominating the market by positioning yourself as an expert

- Focus your marketing

- Know your customers – love your customers

- Service your customers so that you become the 'go-to' company for those people.

SHARE YOUR SUCCESS!

Jonathan Jay and SuccessTrack would like to hear of your successes using the marketing advice in this book.

Send your story and how you successfully used a SuccessTrack principle in your business to: **info@successtrackuk.com**

We may contact you to find out more and we might want to feature your story in a newsletter or future book, so please include your contact details.

Have you enjoyed this book?

You can tell us your opinion of this book and we might include it on the SuccessTrack website, so please give us you name and the type of business you run.

Come to a SuccessTrack event

You can come to events for business owners which are held every month – visit the SuccessTrack website for dates and venues.

Tell other Business Owners

Help spread the word to other business owners about SuccessTrack – join our affiliate scheme by visiting **www.successtrackuk.com** and share the success by being paid commissions for your referrals.

TWO MONTHS FREE PREMIUM MEMBERSHIP TO SUCCESSTRACK WORTH £198!

You can join SuccessTrack free for two months, worth £198, just by registering on the SuccessTrack website. For two months, receive top class business building information from the world's leading experts.

Join SuccessTrack free of charge for two months by visiting **www.successtrackuk.com.**

Claim your free SuccessTrack membership plus your New Member Kit – a set of five marketing CD's and a SuccessTrack gift set – your mouse mat, mug, coaster and pad and pen.

It's all yours, free of charge at successtrackuk.com

YOUR'S FREE!